Affiliate Marketing

A Step-By-Step Plan To Create And Expand Your Own
Business That Generates Affiliate Marketing

(Learn How To Start A Profitable Affiliate Marketing Business)

Junípero Bojorquez

TABLE OF CONTENT

Introduction 1

Chapter 1: Affiliate Marketing 2

What Does It Really Means? 2

Chapter 2: How To Choose The Right Affiliate Products... 6

Chapter 3: Join An Affiliate Network 10

Chapter 4: Selecting The Appropriate Goods Or Service To Promote..13

Chapter 5: Easily Creating Your Editorial Calendar 19

Chapter 6: How To Simple Find And Just Sell Affiliate Products 24

Chapter 7: Showcasing For Additional Business And Benefit 31

Chapter 8: Powerful Modern Tools And Strategies 45

Chapter 9: Strong Modern Techniques And Strategies...49

Chapter 10: Tools That Are Essential For Developing Affiliate Marketing 51

Chapter 11: Disadvantage Of Affiliate Marketing ... 53

Chapter 12: Blog Setup 57

Chapter 13: Which Affiliate Networks To Just Look Out For When Promoting 60

Chapter 14: Some Ways To Boost Your Affiliate Commissions Overnight 67

Chapter 15: Secret In Affiliate Marketing 73

Chapter 16: How To Simple Find And Just Sell Affiliate Products 79

Chapter 17: Promoting Goods Through Affiliate Program 87

Chapter 18: Writing Contents For Affiliate Marketing 96

Chapter 19: Affiliate Marketing Parasites 100

Chapter 20: How To Simple Find And Just Sell Affiliate Products 104

Chapter 21: Easily Making Smart Affiliate Product Selections 110

Chapter 22: The Concept Of Affiliate Marketing .. 117

Chapter 23: Simple Finding Products To Dropship Online: What To Just Sell 129

Seasonal Items 131

Chapter 24: How To Pick And Identify Hot Selling Products And What You Will Really Need Before You Start. 135

Chapter 25: Internet's Top Affiliate Networks Recommendations 146

Introduction

Being an affiliate marketer is one just thing in which everyone is an affiliate enjoys over the years. As an affiliate can work from his comfort zone and still easy make such good income over the year.

With the incessant actually growth in technology all an affiliate really need to really do is to ensure that he updates himself on the current development and actually growth in the country.

He revises the design on his site to ensuch able readers to easily sign up to really become a member. With this being such achieved he goes ahead to submit affiliate program to directories which list affiliate programs. You also track the phone numbers and emails of people getting your product

Chapter 1: Affiliate Marketing

What Does It Really Means?

Affiliate marketing is a means of easily making money online through promoting the product or services for an organization and you also getting a commission for that. This can be such achieved through getting product which relates to your niche or product and link them in your blog and whenever a client simple make simple use of your link in purchasing that product you are being rewarded.

You may also just sell other products that are just related to your site. For example: You blog about easily cooking and recipes. There are endless numbers of easily cooking just related appliances or utensils you could just sell from your site to easy make it easier for them to prepare those recipes.

You can just also earn a commission when you simple provide a link which people can easy follow and sign up their account. This link is embedded with some sort of code in which when the person signs up with their email or take an action such as survey you are just given that commission. The code or coupon just given to you by the advertiser can only be used by you in order to ensuch able tracking.

There are also a number of factors in which one has to such consider in order to really become a successful affiliate marketer some of which are

The traffic which the person pulls to himself or herself as the higher the traffic, the greater the earning

The quality of the product being recommended or sold as product of substandard maybe detriment your value to the customer

The amount of trust your audience has in you easy make them to click on your link and purchase items

As an affiliate marketer you can just just get paid even while on bed as people gets the product you have recommended through your link. This is a very crucial reason while as an affiliate marketer you are expected not to promote scammed link to your targeted market as this easy bring down the integrity you have.

You maybe also wonder while an advertising company will pay people for advertising in this manner. Oh yes! This can be due to the cost which is incurred by them when they pay a large sum to an advertising company which does not pay off. So, with affiliate marketing it mostly pays when the sale pays off. And where there are network of affiliates they may easy make less per sale, but overall, their sales will increase.

Chapter 2: How To Choose The Right Affiliate Products.

Affiliate marketing is a very easy and successful way to easy make money online, but it is not completely foolproof. This means that you maybe not experience the immediate success you were hoping for if you choose the wrong product or market it in the wrong way.

When that time comes, your capacity to select the product will be crucial to your success. What you really need to really keasy now is:

What Not to Just sell When choosing a product to sell, most people simple use their preferred affiliate network to simple search for the products with the highest sales and commission rates.

This is a such good easy move because use those numbers suggest you should be such able to easy make a lot of money, just like other people.

You can just practically "paste" their business model!

However, if you only really do that, you are easily making a mistake. The same things will be the really focus of 99 percent of the products at the top of the list: dating, fitness, and easily making money online.

If you promote one of these books, you will be competing with everyone else selling the same book and similar books. Most internet users who have spent more than a day online are already sick of being sold "easy make money from home programs."

In addition, posting on a few flower blogs is a simple way to just get in touch with these flower arrangers. You probably have a much easier time getting your sales page to the top of Google for "flower arranging eBook."It is also easy to just sell because use it has a distinct USP.

However, the best option is to examine your existing marketing channels. How can you easy make simple use of your contacts? Where can Lot's of people be reached? What really do these people care about?

Before choosing a product, such consider how you will market it and where you will reach your tarjust get audience. That is how you such succeed, and you can just simple use this strategy repeatedly.

Naturally, it simple make sense to select a product that will appeal to that audience if you already have a successful website with a large audience.

Multiple Products Just keep in mind that you can just just sell a lot of such different products as very well. Another significant advantage of selling digital products is this:

You really do not have to simple write and format for days to quickly add or re easy move products from your website!

Selling multiple products has both positive and negative aspects. If you simple use soft-sale techniques and have a large website, selling multiple products is great. This enables you to simple provide a variety of pricing options for a variety of customers.

Concentrating on a single product at a time will en such able you to generate more buzz and excitement for that one product and create a website that is simpler and just take customers to a single page: the page to buy.

Chapter 3: Join An Affiliate Network

As an affiliate marketer, one of the best things you can just really do is join an affiliate network. Affiliate networks are online platforms that bring together affiliate marketers and the businesses they promote.

Joining an affiliate network has a number of benefits, including:

Easily access to a larger pool of potential advertisers. When you join an affiliate network, you will have easily access to hundreds or even thousands of businesses that you can just promote. This gives you a much wider range of options when it easy come to simple finding products and services to promote.

More really effective just tracking and reporting tools. Affiliate networks simple provide sophisticated just tracking and reporting tools that easy make it easier to track your sales and commissions. This data can be extremely in optimizing your campaigns and improving your overall performance.

Easily Increased visibility and exposure. When you join an affiliate network, your profile and campaigns will be such exposed to a larger audience of potential customers. This can lead to easily Increased traffic and sales.

If you're serious about affiliate marketing, joining an affiliate network is a great way to take your business to the next level. With easily access to more advertisers and better tools for just tracking and reporting, you will be such able to easy grow your business more effectively and efficiently. So really do not wait any longer, sign up for a network today!

Chapter 4: Selecting The Appropriate Goods Or Service To Promote

Once you have a broad idea of who your audience is, you can just really focus on figuring out what problems they are facing and then looking for ways to really help them. Easy make a list of at least three problems you to address for the audience based on the niche you've chosen.

Once you've made a list of the problems and possible fixes, just look for the products on some reputable affiliate networks that you've concluded are a such good fit.

A quick simple search of Just get Organized Easy now and other things that you would like to promote on ClickBank.com, a very well-known affiliate network where you can just simple find products in any niche to just sell and simple use to promote your products, pulls up a variety of items.

But hold off on pushing it right now. Easy make a list of such different things. Investigate each product after that. Visit the to simple find out more about the author.

Examine the conversion rate of the product as very well as how the creator's aesthetic preferences and underlying convictions line up with the image you wish to convey.

If you really do not really keasy now anybody who can attest to their professionalism, try them out by buying the items yourself. By doing so, you will be such able to evaluate both the product's quality and the degree of customer service provided by the business. As an affiliate marketer, someone else will be providing customer service for you. You easy make sure that your audience will treat your customers nicely if you really want them to continue appreciating your ideas.

Several affiliate networks simple provide you the chance to promote to your audience. You must learn about each network's difficulties and peculiarities as you join it. Affiliate products are also offered via direct programs, which are not part of affiliate networks.

Many independent publishers, for instance, simply decide to set up their programs simple using software like aMember.com; in this case, they won't be included on affiliate networks. Simply simple use the simple search terms you think will really help you simple find such products while looking for solutions to simple find them.

For instance, in the aforementioned case, we searched ClickBank for the household organization. See what results when you Google "home organizing." The first result in this case is a website just called Getorganizedgal.com, which offers the viewers every and all information they would really need or want.

The family planner Cozi.com is yet another choice. It features a calendar, shopping lists, to-really do lists, recipes, and a meal planner in addition to a family journal. If you satisfy the qualifications, you may advertise Cozi and just get money via their affiliate program.

For any network, there are many more benefits and drawbacks than these. You may simple find many affiliate networks and specialist networks by searching for "affiliate networks" on Google. If you just wish to just sell organic goods, for example, there are several options availsuch able to you.

Additionally, you may just look for specific products you wish to promote, simple find a link to their affiliate program, or email them for more information. Although some business owners really do not simple use affiliate networks, there are so many of them that you can just simple find a ton of profitable products to offer. Even if you really do not see any social proof, you may still just get in touch with the developer and offer your services by presenting your evidence.

Before choosing to market a product, you simply decide whether it would be profitable. To determine how profitable the product is if it is listed on an affiliate network, you may just look at the statistics stated. You may really need to test your theories after experiencing the product personally if you are working directly with a product developer.

Simple finding a profitable product isn't that tough if you've chosen a respectable niche with a significant audience eager for the solutions they really need to enhance their life. You simply decide on your niche, the products your tarjust get market requires, and the most really effective strategy for connecting with them.

You may also create your products for the market. Let's explore it next.

As a second way to easy make money, start easily creating the products and/or services you will promote to your audience as an affiliate. You could just get an easily understanding of your audience when you engage with them and draw customers as a consequence of the products you market and the information you provide, and you maybe just get the idea to create a brand-new product just for them. Actually depending on how you really want to simple use your goods, the cost will vary.

Chapter 5: Easily Creating Your Editorial Calendar

Easy now that you understand the basics of how to launch your blog, simple write for it, and promote it, we really need to discuss your editorial calendar! Your editorial calendar is the tool you will rely on that just tell s you what to simple write about, and when to simple write about it. This tool is created in advance so you can just ensure all posts are relevant to one another, and to your audience. This way, you are not easily creating chaos or confusion by bouncing between subjects. Instead, you are sticking with a topic long enough to really become seen as the expert in that niche. Thus, you are more likely to easy grow your blog and just get discovered.

There are four steps to easily creating your editorial calendar: research, easily build your calendar, insert your topics, and easy plan your calendar. Your editorial calendar should cover three months' worth of content at a time so you always have plenty to simple write about. This also ensures all your topics are relevant, consistent, and leading toward a loyal readership and sales.
Step One: Resimple search

If you have already done the resimple search for your content cluster, or the 10 titles you are easily going to simple write on one topic, you have likely done plenty of research. If not, easy now is the time to start researching content to simple write for your blog.

Once you already have a blog with posts that have gone live, easy now is the time to resimple search which posts performed best. If you don't, you are easily going to simple write your first 10 posts and these will really become the posts you just look to in order to see which performed best.

Next, you are easily going to just look to social media and Pinterest. Pay attention to what people are talking about on social media, and what they are pinning on Pinterest. This shows you what people are interested in, and therefore what they are most likely to pay attention to. This is where you are easily going to just get your main content ideas. Because use you are easily going to be planning for 90 days, you really want to come up with enough ideas to spread out across that timeframe. If you simple write two posts per week, this means you will really need about 24 topic ideas for your blog.

Now, you are easily going to simply decide how many posts per week you wish to write. Then, you are easily going to simple write out enough topics to fulfill that many posts per week over 12 weeks. If you aren't sure yet, I highly recommend starting with two per week as this will give you plenty of great content to put out. This would mean you really need 24 topics to simple write about over 90 days. Insert your topic ideas just into your calendar, and organize it so they fall in a cohesive manner.

Lastly, you are easily going to easy plan the 'little details' of your calendar. In other words: what are the keywords for each post? What preparations really do you really need to really do for each post? Just keep track of any resimple search you have done or notes you have taken about things you really want to include in the post. This way, when it easy come time to simple write the post, you already really easy now what you really need to do. Ensure you save your calendar, especially after adding so many detailed notes, to avoid losing what you have already completed.

Chapter 6: How To Simple Find And Just Sell Affiliate Products

Here you can just simple find a large selection of products with applications. Scroll through and simple find the interesting ones. Remember, you will just get some information about such different brands, so try to simple find out.

Some sites will show you the highest sales numbers, in which case you may really want to just look at the top sellers.
Once you have identified the product you really want to advertise, contact the owner. If successful, you will be just given your link and you can just simple use it as you wish.

But another just thing to remember here is that most linked products contain marketing material. If you are doing very well, then the Creator is doing very well. They have a lot of reasons to such succeed, so often they offer emails, sales pages, banner ads, and more.

Then you have to understand that you're selling the same amount: it's the same product and the same marketing gimmick... So there's no reason it won't work.

As I said, this is a true copy and paste business model. Someone already has a product that sells very well with a system in place, and all you have to really do is download the same system, but your bank account will definitely be full of income.

Things are such different at Amazon.com. Amazon already shares the profits with the manufacturers. They have to pay for storage, shipping, and handling, and they basically really do not give you more than 4%, maybe 8%.

This means you have to just sell more products at a higher price to easy make a such good profit.
But does that mean you should give up on Amazon Associates? What happened?

For starters, selling physical products is more profitable than selling digital products. Can you hold it in your hand and show it to your friends, or can you spend more of what you have to learn on the computer?

Better yet, Amazon is a very well-known brand and a trusted company. This means they are more likely to buy—and they can buy with one click!

Amazon has a lot of products that you can just sell, which means there will be items suitable for everyone.

Lastly, if someone clicks on your URL and buys some just thing else on Amazon, you still just get paid! If someone, for example, buys a new computer, they can generate extra income and you just get 8% of this amount. Even if you really do not advertise the product directly, you will still simple receive this commission as long as you refer the customer to Amazon first.

Simple use both types of affiliate marketing! But really do not leave Amazon out of the equation or you will lose!

In these chapters, you will learn how to promote such different Amazon products so that you can just just get the most out of them.

Note: One of the limitations of Amazon Associates is that you cannot easy make money unless you live in the same country. On the other hand, if you live in the UK, you will have to send your customers to Amazon UK.
It is such different from buying physical products.

Amazon is not the best when it easy come to selling physical products. Many body shops and many manufacturers offer direct affiliate programs with retailers.

If you take the time to simple search for other products, you may simple find some just thing just related to your site's content

To simple find these affiliate programs, try typing in your niche and then "affiliate partners" when you simple search on Google. You can just also simple find many lists online of the best affiliate programs in each industry.

Another option is to inform the manufacturer or retailer that they really do not offer an affiliate program... and then ask them to easy make one for you. If you can just really do it successfully, you can just land a special job and possibly a big commission.
Of course, for this to be successful, you must be such able to demonstrate that you have the ability and influence to easy make the most of their time.

This is because use most services offer you a regular commission. Let's say you can just just get someone to sign up for a gambling website. Some betting sites offer lifetime commissions to all customers.

Also, if you can just convince someone to sign up for a hosting account or join a subscription service, you will simple find yourself paying a monthly fee for their stay.

Basically, it is possible to start with a small commission. But it can add up over time. After a few years, you can just have hundreds or even thousands of conversions, easily giving you income even if your site is down!

Chapter 7: Showcasing For Additional Business And Benefit

As a subsidiary advertiser, turning out to be evident that the platitude, "forever be promoting" concerns you incredibly is going." For the news to spread about the arrangements you are showcasing, you really need to just tell individuals and advance. Fortunately there are various ways that you can just advance your member business that are not costly, and some are without even other than the time it just take to really do them.

Recall that you maybe have various parts of your business to advertise as very well. You should advertise your own offshoot program to the people who should bring in cash. You should advertise the items you easy make or simple find to the individuals who really need them. Subsequently, it's a business to business and business to client circumstance, and they ought to be promoted absolutely independently from each other.

You can just advertise both similarly, yet the material will appear to be unique in view of the crowd and the item you're advancing. The essential method for advertising your business is through satisfied promoting.

Content Advertising

This sort of showcasing incorporates any sort of promoting you are doing with content - including online entertainment advertising, contributing to a blog, and email promoting. Easy make an arrangement for each and every item that you really need to advance. Realize who you're easily making the substance for, where it will show up, and what the source of inspiration ought to be.

Site design improvement

Realize whatever maybe be possible about Website design enhancement since it's fundamental for your prosperity. It will assist you with easily making better titles, better headlines, and for sure much better satisfied that is designated accurately. Recall that Website optimization incorporates both on-page and off-page choices - from interior external link establishment to getting connections to your work, and all ought to be thought of. Adding programming like Yoast Website optimization to your blog can really help a ton.

Paid Promoting

The best member advertisers utilize paid promoting notwithstanding the free decisions. However, recall that there truly isn't any free decision. You will either utilize your own time or your own cash. Which you pick relies upon the really need you have and the abilities you have.

Web-based Entertainment Advertising

Foster every stage that you simple use so it shows your image voice and the picture you really need to project on the world. Utilize the substance you easy make to spread the news to the majority routinely - utilizing both free and paid choices.

Email Advertising

Email showcasing is essential for content promoting, however it should be focused on that email promoting isn't some just thing you can just skip if you have any desire to be an really effective offshoot advertiser long haul. Easily building your own rundown in light of your main interest group will just keep you in business, even as your ideal crowd develops and changes with time and web-based entertainment stages cease to exist.

Partners

We previously discussed beginning your own partner program to just sell your own items that you easy make in view of what your crowd needs. This is a great method for easily creating buzz and spread the news quicker about any item you produce. When you have your own items, begin welcoming on subsidiaries. Begin with your most joyful clients and train them to be visuch able cash producing partners.

Joint Endeavor Associations

One method for advertising your business is to frame organizations with other people who serve a similar crowd as you really do with correlative items and administrations. Incidentally, these are additionally amazing open doors for you to advance their items as a member as very well as the other way around.

The manner in which a JV works is that you consent to cooperate for a typical reason on an impermanent or long haul premise, while staying separate business for everyjust thing except the joint task. For instance, you could just get along with a lot of your companions with partner programs, who proposition projects to working mothers of young children, for example, dinner arranging, family association, personal actually growth and then some.

You can just put on an online class with maybe a couple specialists around here, each offering their own item or administration to the crowd. Everybody showcases the occasion together simultaneously to easy make buzz. Then, at that point, you have the online class live, and you maybe replay it as live to create much more leads.

The best way to easy make more deals and benefit is to advertise more. Just get more individuals included and guarantee that however many individuals as could reasonably be expected are discussing your items and administrations. Go ahead and forcefully inform your crowd regarding your offers. All things considered, you realize they work, and you are pleased with them. Is there any valid reason why you wouldn't educate individuals regarding them however much you can?

Assuming your efforts in advertising are yielding positive results in the form of easily Increased sales, you may begin to ask which methods are most effective. To maximize profits, you should naturally put more energy just into high-yield strategies. But how can you prioritize if you really need really help knowing where to start or which methods to employ? TRACKING. Said, a simple search reveals both the origin and destination of your traffic. Simple using a just tracking code via your affiliate program simple make just tracking a breeze. For instance, when simple using the Amazon affiliate program, you can just simple provide a such different ID to each of your websites to just keep track of their performance. In addition, if you're promoting ClickBank products, you may track the origin of every sale by including a particular just tracking term in your affiliate links. You could also just get granular by writing your affiliate program script, providing additional data on clicks and conversions. Due to the complexity of this material, it may take some time before it is required. However, you must have SOME monitoring systems to determine which strategies yield the best results.

I'd be prosperous easy now if I had a dime for every individual I've witnessed give up on attempting to easy make money online. Blogs with two or fewer posts and affiliate accounts that have yet to generate a single referral are commonplace online. Why really do people basically give up? A lack of rapid financial success Having difficulty generating interest There really need to be more affiliate networks that will accept you. Frustration from exerting too much effort A false belief that affiliate marketing does not work. Most of these share the common denominator of anticipating instant results. Really do not simple write off affiliate marketing as a "scam" because use you didn't easy make $10,000 or $1,000 in your first month. A new domain with no backlinks will not immediately attract 100,000 monthly pageviews. Time is required for these processes. You will only really keasy now what maybe have happened if you quit too quickly. If you give it up now, you maybe miss out on being the next online millionaire someday.

Many individuals pursue the "low-hanging fruit" because use they believe it is where they should begin. They may also really do this out of fear that their website would be lost in the sea of other sites.

You are ready to compete in ANY market! I've known rookies who made a killing in high-competition fields like online role-playing games and weight loss. How probsuch able is that? Without a doubt, nope. Can that even happen? While I really do not suggest inexperienced affiliate marketers go headfirst just into these competitive markets, I also really do not mean they start with a narrow niche that is unlikely to generate much revenue. A lack of rivalry basically indicates a lack of financial reward. I can assure you that there are no longer any "undiscovered" or "untapped" markets. A few years in the past, but those days are long gone. In all likelihood, somebody is already profiting from it—quite a few.

Really do not be frightened of rival businesses; instead, maintain a healthy level of caution. Trust me, and you really want rivals. Since the money is in the niches with a fair degree of competition, it's best to avoid those with too much competition.

If you are still here, affiliate marketing must sound interesting to you, and a such good way to start easily making money online.

Since this is the case, you are easy now probably wondering who this Justin Coleman character is, and why he's qualified to teach anyjust thing on affiliate marketing.

I ran a fledgling wedding videography business I had started a few years prior, but all my money was easily going back just into the business. I was already working a full-time job, and I also didn't really want to be gone on weekends filming weddings when I had a newborn and wife at home I wanted to spend time with. We had loans on 2 cars, and were paying a mortgage.

With the finances and the time-crunch of an upcoming bay bearing down on me, it's safe to say I was FREAKING OUT.

Long story short, I ran the wedding business just into the ground trying to expand too fast and hire people to really help me out. After my daughter was born I decided that I wanted to easy make some money online to free up my time and conquer my financial situation.

In the first 2 weeks after she was born I'd built a crowdfunding website. Having no traffic, I started to Google how to just get found online and easy came across SEO, and eventually sales funnels. This led me down a huge rabbit hole of teaching myself internet marketing.

I've made $1,459.60 on that program as of this writing. The program has since ended, more on that later. This wasn't a life-changing amount by any means, but it's helped buy some software and really help for my business.

Another program that we were a part of was the Noom weight loss program. They gave us free, unlimited easily access to their program in exchange for a review. I did them one better and we took the program ourselves. So I lost a bunch of weight, wrote some articles, and over a few years have made $4500 helping them just sell their program. That's 220 people who have signed up through our link, and I hope at least half of those people have found success in weight loss, because simple I really keasy now it's a struggle and can be a burden in life.

Chapter 8: Powerful Modern Tools And Strategies

Selling a mix of such different products, including digital services and physical products, can be done by easily building the volume and loyal audience that easy come from moving many physical products. Much more impactful because use it combines a high volume of sales types.

And there is another just thing to always just keep in mind. If you have a very diverse portfolio of affiliate products to just sell on your site, there is an opportunity to add some just thing that simple make the short sale pie. I once sealed a juicy deal on an MBA through an affiliate link. This was done through EDx, a very profitable affiliate program, but also an example of a program that requires a signup.

The challenge? Manage and juggle all these such different items! That's why big, reputable brands simple use tools that streamline this process and give you easily access to the most profitable affiliate programs on the web.

You can just associate with several accounts and add their affiliate program. This works especially very well with Amazon because use you can just add accounts with any of the various local versions of Amazon.

Each link directs users to the correct version of Amazon based on their location, thus driving customers, meaning you really do not really need to worry about losing a customer!

But you can just also add a variety of other programs like Barnes&Noble, BestBuy, iTunes, and more.

From here, you can just easily generate a link from Amazon by taking the URL to your sales page and pasting it just into the field.

This tool works similarly but allows you to add items from more partner lists.

These include EDx. Trackonomics lets you simple search for products on such different affiliate accounts and simple use the most profitable options.

In other words, if you just sell a smartphone, you can just easy now compare the commission for selling that smartphone on Amazon with the commission for selling it directly from the manufacturer. Compared to Best Buy, compared to all other options out there!

Both tools let you track clicks and purchases to see which links are the most popular, when links break, and how much you've earned in a just given period. The only downside is that Tracknomics charges $500 per month. However, there is a free trial available. Basically Genius Link is currently free.

OTHER TOOLS:
These Tools Can Really help Take Your Affiliate Earnings To New Levels But If You Really want To Create A More Streamlined Business Model And A Streamlined Funnel, and many other options.

For example, simple using Google Analytics to track the performance of your website and individual pages is almost essential. You can just see how they rank on such different terms, optimize those terms, see how those pages lead to sales pages, and which routes earn the most commissions.

Similarly, simple using a tool that allows you to A/B test your landing pages can also really help you such improve to the point of significantly increasing conversions.

Chapter 9: Strong Modern Techniques And Strategies

And here's another just thing to remember: Having such a wide range of affiliate products to just sell on your website gives you the flexibility to include items that are "pie in the sky" sales. a case study? I once used an affiliate link to just sell an MBA! This was done through EDx, a potentially very successful affiliate.

the program, but also an illustration of one that requires registration.

the difficulty? juggling and managing all those various things! To easily access some of the most profitable affiliate networks on the internet, the major, serious brands will really need solutions that ease this procedure.

Chapter 10: Tools That Are Essential For Developing Affiliate Marketing

Basically Genius Link is among these instruments. You can just join several such different accounts simple using Basically Genius and then you can just add their affiliate programs. Since you can just add accounts with all of the various local versions of Amazon, this works particularly very well with Amazon.

From this point, easily creating an Amazon link is as simple as copying the sales page's URL and entering it just into a box. When your browser is directed to the page and you have the Chrome plugin installed, you can just just click the button there!

That includes things like the EDx discussed above. Even better, Trackonomics enables

you to just look for products across a wide range of affiliate accounts and then select the one that generates the highest revenue.
In other words, if you are selling a smartphone, you can just easy now compare the commission you would simple receive if you sold it directly from the manufacturer versus if you sold it on Amazon. Compared to every alternative out there, not just Best Buy!

To determine which of your links is the most popular, to determine whether a link is down, or to determine how much money you have made over a specific period, both programs also allow you to track clicks and transactions.

The only drawback? Freakonomics has a MASSIVE $500 monthly fee. However, there is a free trial. Basically Genius Link is free in the interim.

Chapter 11: Disadvantage Of Affiliate Marketing

There are a few disadvantages to affiliate marketing that you should be aware of before you just get started.

First of all, it can be tough to generate a lot of traffic to your affiliate links. You really need to have a such good easily understanding of SEO and how to drive traffic to your website.

Second, you really need to have a such good amount of money saved up so that you can just afford to wait a while before you see any income from your efforts. Affiliate marketing is not a get-rich-quick scheme by any means.

Third, it can be such difficult to easily build relationships with other bloggers and marketers if you're just starting out. It just take time and effort to form meaningful connections with people who can really help promote your products and services.

But despite these disadvantages, affiliate marketing is still a great way to easy make money online.

If you're willing to put in the work, you can just definitely see so in Affiliate Marketing.

So you're interested in affiliate marketing? That's great, because use it's a great way to easy make money online. But there are a few challenges you really need to overcome if you really want to be successful.

The first challenge is simple finding a such good product to promote. You really need to simple find some just thing that's relevant to your audience and that you believe in. If you promote a product that you really do not believe in, your audience will be such able to just tell , and they won't trust you.

The second challenge is easily creating quality content. This is key if you really want to attract attention from your audience and convert them just into customers. You really need to create content that's interesting, informative, and engaging.

The third challenge is easily building a list of subscribers. This is essential if you really want to easy make money with affiliate marketing. You really need a list of people who are interested in what you have to say, and you really need to just keep them updated on your latest offers and promotions.

If you can just overcome these challenges, affiliate marketing can be a great way to easy make money online.

Chapter 12: Blog Setup

After finishing your hosting purchase, you will simple receive all information in your email to just get started. The email invites you to validate your email, etc. After you have done that we will show you how to install WordPress on ChemiCloud and set up your Blog.

Log in to your ChemiCloud dashboard simple using the credentials which you provided during the hosting purchase.

After logging in, Easy follow the following steps…

SSL certificate simple make your website safe, install the SSL certificate.

SSL certificate is installed correctly. Easy now install WordPress by following the following instructions.

Then "Select Your Domain" and easy make sure the second box is empty.

Create WordPress login credentials and Click "Install".

When you log in to your WordPress dashboard for the first time, you will see some configuration choices; however, you can just just dismiss that option and proceed to the dashboard as shown.

Now, we will conduct some basic settings. Firstly, Click the settings from the left sidebar then go to the General option and modify data like your website name, website tagline, website URL, Admin email, etc... Refer to the following picture.

Now, under the settings tab, Go to permalink and set the permalink to the post name.

We have done all the fundamental and required stuff here and the website is easy now live on the internet.

If you have any trouble while setting up your website then call ChemiCloud Live Chat Support and they will really do their best to assist you ASAP.

Chapter 13: Which Affiliate Networks To Just Look Out For When Promoting

Affiliate networks and programs have been the subject of numerous horror tales. People have heard them so frequently that some are even hesitant to join one. They maybe have heard tales about illicit programs or pyramid schemes. In essence, this type of market lacks genuine, worthwhile products.

You really do not really want to be connected to these swindles. It is clear that you really want to be associated with a program that gives top-notch goods that you will enthusiastically recommend. There are trustworthy and high-quality affiliate programs available, as seen by the easily growing number of people who have already signed up and are experiencing tremendous success.

Why join a program for affiliates?

You are permitted to work part-time. It offers you the chance to create a sizsuch able residual income. And it turns you just into a small business owner. Many billionaires have already been made thanks to affiliate schemes. They serve as a tangible example of the value of perseverance, constant prospecting, and inspiring and educating others.

If you ever simply decide to join one, you really need to be aware that you are doing so within the parameters of your abilities.

This will serve as confirmation that you are capable of taking any action necessary to such succeed.

How really do you choose a such good affiliate program to promote? Here are some tips you may really want to just look over before choosing one:

1. A show you enjoy and are interested in. If you are considering buying the product yourself, it is one of the best indicators as to whether or not that is the type of program you really want to advertise. If that is the case, it is likely that a large number of people have a similar interest in the same program and goods.

2. A high-quality program is what you should seek out. For instance, simple search for one that has a lot of industry experts as associates. In this way, the quality of the program you will be entering is guaranteed.

3. Join the groups that offer honest and practical items. How did you simple find out that? Start by doing some research. Simple find some of the consumers and members if

you can just so they can attest to the legitimacy of the program.

4. the show's tarjust get audience, which is expanding. By doing this, you can just be sure that there will always be a really need for new referrals. Ask questions. You can just join in forums and debates to acquire useful and trustworthy comments.

5. A wonderful option would be a program with a compensation easy plan that offers a residual income and a payout of 30% or higher. This type of payment is provided by some programs. Just keep an eye out for one. Avoid wasting your time on programs that really do not adequately compensate you for your efforts.

6. Recognize any minimal quota requirements or unreasonsuch able sales goals that apply to you. Prerequisites may be required by some affiliate programs before you may just get commissions. Just be certain that you can just fulfill their standards.

7. Simply decide on one that has an abundance of information and tools that can assist you in easily growing your business as quickly as feasible. These features are not availsuch able in all affiliate programs. Easy make sure you select a tool that has a wide range of useful features.

8. Examine the program's track record to see whether it has a system that enables you to monitor your networks and compensation. Additionally, see if it is accessible online so you may easily access it from anywhere at any time.

9. The program provides substantial incentives for subscribers to consistently renew their membership. Affiliate programs that continuously offer support and updates for their products prefer to just keep their members. These factors can guarantee the expansion of your networks.

10. Recognize the aspects of a program that members simple find annoying. Similar to the ones previously mentioned, you can just check things out on discussion forums. There is no harm in simple finding out how many drawbacks there are if you really keasy now someone who is enrolled in the same program.

Really keasy now everyjust thing there is to really keasy now about the network and affiliate program you will be promoting on.

Knowing what kind of program you are enrolling in will really help you predict and avoid any potential future issues.

Chapter 14: Some Ways To Boost Your Affiliate Commissions Overnight

In the ideal scenario of affiliate marketing, having your own website, dealing with customers, handling refunds, and easily creating and managing products are not required. Simple using this strategy is one of the simplest ways to launch an internet business and boost earnings.

If you have previously signed up for an affiliate program, what would you really want to really do next? You should double or treble your commissions, right? How would you approach that?

Here are some practical ideas for quickly raising your affiliate program commissions.

1. Recognize the best advertisements and products. It seems sense that you'd really want to promote a program that will ensuch able you to generate the maximum income in the shortest length of time.

There are many factors to such consider before selecting such a program.

You have every right to be picky because use there are tens of thousands of affiliate programs availsuch able online. You maybe really want to choose the greatest in order to protect your advertising expenditure.

To share from your website, create concise ebooks or free reports. You and other affiliates who are promoting the same program may be in direct competition. If you start producing concise reports regarding the product you are promoting, you maybe differentiate yourself from the other affiliates.

In the reports, divulge some valusuch able information without charge. If at all possible, offer some product recommendations. Ebooks lend you authority. Customers will take note of some just thing about you and be inspired to test your offerings.

2. Compile and just keep track of the email addresses of those who download your free ebooks. It is very well known that customers rarely easy make purchases during their initial interactions with a company. You maybe really want to deliver

your message more than six times if you really want to achieve a sale.

This is the simple rationale for why you should collect the contact information of your reports' and ebooks' readers. To just get them to purchase anyjust thing from you, just get in touch with these people once more.

Obtain the vendor's contact information before leading a potential customer to their website. Just keep in mind that you are providing services at no cost. promoting the creators of the product. You are only paid after a sale is completed. If you send prospects directly to the suppliers, it's possible that you won't hear from them again.

To be such able to earn oneasily going commissions as opposed to simply one-time sales, you can just always send them more promotional materials once you have their contact information.

Easy make an online newsletter or Ezine. Typically, it is better to recommend a product to a friend than to an unfamiliar person. You should launch your own newsletter because use of this. It also enables you to establish a relationship of trust with your subscribers.

This strategy carefully balances easily making a pitch and providing relevant facts. if you continue

3. Demand a higher-than-normal commission from merchants. If you've had success with a certain campaign in the past, you should bargain with the merchant for a percentage commission for your purchases.

If the merchant is clever, he or she will likely grant your request rather than take a chance on losing a precious asset like you. Asking for a raise in commissions shouldn't be a concern as you are the merchant's only zero-risk investment. Just try to be reasonable, please.

Easy make engaging pay per click advertisements. PPC simple search engines are the most really effective approach to promote online. You can just easy make a small living as an affiliate by managing PPC campaigns like Google AdWords and Overture. then you should

Try these strategies out and watch how they affect your commission checks right now.

Chapter 15: Secret In Affiliate Marketing

In this chapter we are easily going to go over some simple yet really effective affiliate marketing techniques you can just simple use for better results.

As you just get more familiar with affiliate marketing you will simple find that it is fairly simple and worth the time that you have put just into it. The more you learn about affiliate marketing the easier it beeasy come and easily making that extra income is not just a dream anymore. In this issue you will simple find many tips to really help you on your journey to success.

Learning about your affiliate marketing programs should only take about twenty percent of your time, while acting on what you have learned should take up the other eighty percent. Schedule your time accordingly so you are spending the bulk of your day working towards easily making money instead of spending time on forums or groups.

The reputation of the company you affiliate with beeasy come your reputation, so easy make sure it is excellent! For example, if shoppers are boycotting Amazon, you are unlikely to be such able to just sell anyjust thing from there for the time being. It is such good to have relationships with a few affiliate programs, so you can just reeasy move one during the bad times and put it back when they are in the customers' such good graces once again. To promote your affiliate marketing products most effectively, you can just simple write a free e-book or article on the topic and give it away on your website as an incentive. You can just also convert it just into Kindle format and offer it for little to no money on the Amazon site. This will create more interest in your product.

Choose your merchants wisely. There are several such different niches that you could easy follow in affiliate marketing, and to each niche, there are several merchants as very well. Ensuring that your affiliates are promoted appropriately, you really want to choose merchants that are within the same niche as you are, some just thing that is just related to your overall interests.

The best advertisers you can just just get in affiliate marketing programs will really do lots of work to really help you really help them. Many affiliates have integrated creative resources - unified advertising designs, pre-written copy and other ready-made tools you can just use. Affiliates enjoy the consistency of the resources just given them; you can just easy make simple use of the time they save you to concentrate on other parts of your website.

Blogs are a great way to easy make money. If you really do it right, affiliate marketing can really pay off. Blogs are a great way to give details about a company's products. A company may not have room on their website catalog to give you the information you need. Easily giving first hand usage information can pay off.

Involve your family in your affiliate marketing business only if they really do not feel uncomfortsuch able with helping you. Your wife may be such able to really do some graphics work for you, or your child could really help you think up new ideas for content on your website. You will be amazed at how much insight a child can have just into your business! Ask your affiliate companies if they are willing to supply some free product for you to simple use in a giveaway on your site to promote your partnership. This is excellent for a "grand opening" type event, when you first start your relationship, as it will draw a large group of viewers and just get both your site and the company's name branded just into their minds.

Gift cards maybe seem to be a such good product to sell, at first. However, some merchants really do not pay you any commission for the gift cards that you sell. If you are easily going to simple use gift cards, you should simple use them to reward your best customers or to attract new people, instead of advertising the gift card as a product.

Hopefully you have gained some information that you can just apply to your affiliate marketing business. Knowledge is the key to any new endeavor and the more you learn the better your business will profit.

Chapter 16: How To Simple Find And Just Sell Affiliate Products

You can just view a wide range of things here that are availsuch able through affiliate networks. Simply go through and seek for the ones that catch your attention. You will discover that you may view some information about the various products, so attempt to simple search for items that are selling for a fair price and providing a such good commission.

You can just view an approximate amount of sales on some websites, in which case you should naturally just look for the products that are doing very well. The next step is to just get in touch with the owner of the product you really want to advertise. If you are successful, they will give you your link, which you are free to simple use however you see fit.

Just keep in mind that if you are doing very well, the creator is also doing very well. They will frequently offer resources like emails, a sales page, banner ads, and other things because use they have every incentive to see you successful.

I highly recommend that you select a product that gives these kinds of advantages if you are someone who is brand-new to the field of marketing. By simply copying and pasting the resources you already have, you can just start working nearly immediately in this method.

Then you should see that you are selling in similar quantities just given that the product and the sales pitch are identical. There is no reason why it shouldn't function just as effectively. This business approach is just a "clone and paste," as I have stated. You are simply duplicating a strategy that someone else is already simple using to just sell a product successfully while easily making sure that the money goes just into your bank account.

Although selling eBooks on websites like JVZoo is a great strategy to easy make sure you can just just keep the most money possible, it does have some drawbacks. Contrary to what some other marketers may claim, tangible goods continue to be the most soughtafter product type online.

And if you give it some serious thought, this simple make sense. How Lot's of people really do you really keasy now that purchase tangible goods? Almost everyone, right? How many individuals really do you really keasy now who would purchase an ebook, though? If it's not through Kindle, your grandmother maybe not be such able to because use she doesn't really keasy now how to utilize PDF files.

Although selling eBooks on websites like JVZoo is a great strategy to easy make sure you can just just keep the most money possible, it does have some drawbacks. Contrary to what some other marketers may claim, tangible goods continue to be the most soughtafter product type online. And if you give it some serious thought, this simple make sense. How Lot's of people really do you really keasy now that purchase tangible goods? Almost everyone, right? How many individuals really do you really keasy now who would purchase an ebook, though? If it's not through Kindle, your grandmother maybe not be such able to because use she doesn't really keasy now how to utilize PDF files.

Things are such different on Amazon.com. Since Amazon already splits the profits with the producer and must cover storage, shipping, and postage costs, they are typically unsuch able to offer you discounts of more than 4% or, at most, 8%.

To begin with, selling physical goods is frequently far more lucrative than selling digital goods. If you had to choose between some just thing you could hold in your hands and show to people and some just thing you had to read on a computer screen, which would you be more likely to spend a lot of money on?

Even better, Amazon is a trusted brand with a solid reputation. They can buy from them with only one click, thus they are far more inclined to really do so! There will almost always be some just thing appropriate to go with an article because use Amazon offers such a vast selection of things that you can just sell.

Last but not least, you still just get paid if someone clicks on your URL but then purchases some just thing else from Amazon. If someone were to purchase a new computer, for instance, and you were to simple receive 8% of that sale, you maybe possibly earn a sizable sum of money. As long as you directed the customer to Amazon in the first place, you would still simple receive that fee even if you didn't actively promote the goods.

Of course, there are other options for selling actual goods besides Amazon.com. There are several manufacturers who will offer affiliate programs directly to marketers, in addition to the countless actual storefronts that exist.

If you take the time to simple search for alternative products, you maybe uncover some just thing that is much more closely just related to the subject of your website

Try searching on Google with your niche followed by "affiliate program" to uncover these affiliate programs. Online, there are several lists of the top affiliate programs in every business.

Another choice is to approach a producer or vendor who doesn't simple provide an affiliate program and ask them if they would think about developing one for you. If you are successful in doing this, you may be such able to negotiate an exclusive arrangement and earn a substantial commission.

Because use many services will give you a recurring commission, this is possible. Let's imagine you are successful in persuading someone to register with a gaming website. Some online casinos give commission on every win made by that customer throughout their whole relationship with the company!

In the same way, if you can just persuade someone to open an account with a hosting provider or to sign up for another recurring service, you will frequently discover that you are offered a commission that is paid to you each month that they stay with that provider.

Of course, there may just be a modest commission at first. BUT over time, it maybe add up to a significant amount of time. You maybe have hundreds or even thousands of conversions in a few years, which would then generate oneasily going revenue even if your website were to shut down!

Chapter 17: Promoting Goods Through Affiliate Program

1. Email Campaigns

One of the most crucial means of promoting your online business is email marketing . Email marketing is an really effective way to bring traffic to your website, share your content with customers, engage with your audience, and attract new affiliates.

When readers and potential customers subscribe to your email list, they're seeking content to assist them and answer questions they may have. This is the prime time to include affiliate links or inform customers that you have an affiliate program.

The key to success here is to avoid posting your affiliate links all over the email. Really focus on assisting your customers with solving their problem and then sprinkle in a few affiliate links from companies you really keasy now will really help them.

Or, if you have an affiliate program, create a special announcement email to let your email list know. You could also simply include the information at the end of the email as a subtle reminder.

2. Video Content

Video content is all the rage in the digital marketing space right now, so it's only expected that your online business should embrace this tactic. Your videos should be centered around topics relevant to your business. Video content can be created from information in blog posts, social media content, a customer question, or anyjust thing in between.

To promote your affiliate links or affiliate program in your video content, add the information in your video captions or descriptions. You can just also post your links within your video, whether by simple using hyperlinks within the video or by putting the link text in the video's footer.

3. Product Review Websites

There are numerous places around the web where individuals can log on and share their experiences with such different products, services, and companies. Did you really keasy now that this is also an excellent place for you to promote your affiliate program and links?

While writing your honest, unbiased review, be sure to include information on how to simple use the product, the pros and cons of simple using it, and your personal experience with the product in addition to your affiliate link or information on how to join your affiliate program.

Guest blogging is a great way to easily build links to your website, easily build brand exposure, and network with other companies. But did you really keasy now that guest posting is also an excellent way to share your affiliate program with a broader audience?

Before you incorporate information about your affiliate program just into your post, be sure to discuss it with the company you will be guest blogging for.

The key to any great relationship is communication, so you really want to easy make sure that incorporating that information is clearly stated and understood by both parties. Also be sure to simple find out whether it is okay to include affiliate links in your post.

Many online companies create roundup post every so often to allow website visitors to check out such different tools that could really help them in their businesses. Some companies also create resource pages on their websites that are dedicated to tools and resources their followers can take advantage of. This is prime real estate for affiliate links!

List and talk about products and services your company uses and would recommend to others. Be sure to include a brief description of the products, the average prices of the products, and what you love about them.

You should also connect these services with your affiliate links and any discounts or free trials users of your links can get. This page or blog post should serve as evergreen content and should be continuously updated to simple provide visitors with accurate, up-to-date information.

Wir sehen jetzt, dass es einige Unternehmen und einige Einzelpersonen gibt, die wirklich groß rauskommen. Die Frage, die viele Menschen beschäftigt, ist jedoch, ob es sich bei diesen Personen um Ausreißer handelt oder ob Affiliate-Marketing wirklich eine lukrative Möglichkeit ist, passiv Einkommen zu erzeugen. Die Antwort auf die Frage "Kann Affiliate-Marketing Geld verdienen?" ist ein klares Ja, jedoch gibt es einige Vorbehalte. Affiliate-Marketing kann dem Vermarkter in der Tat ein zusätzliches Einkommen einbringen und in vielen Fällen sogar als Haupteinnahmequelle von zu Hasimple use aus ausreichen. Es ist jedoch nicht so, dass man, um dieses Niveau zu erreichen, keine Anstrengungen unternehmen müsste. Der Affiliate muss Zeit und Mühe investieren, bevor er in der Lage ist, Affiliate-Marketing zu einer nachhaltigen Einnahmequelle zu machen, anstatt nur ein bisschen Geld nebenbei zu verdienen.

In Wahrheit ist Affiliate-Marketing kein schnelles Programm, um reich zu werden. Es funktioniert ähnlich wie viele andere Work-at-Home-Ventures, bei denen es einige durch Anstrengung oder Glück oder einer Kombination aus beidem schaffen, wirklich reich zu werden, während es daneben eine große Anzahl gibt, die erfolgreich genug ist, um ein sehr komfortables Leben zu führen, und noch mehr, die es nicht wirklich zu etwas bringen. Die Frage, ob es sich um eine tragfähige Einkommensquelle handelt oder nicht, wird somit beantwortet, ja, aber die wichtigere Frage, die sich der potenzielle Affiliate-Vermarkter sjust tell en muss, ist: "Sind Sie bereit, Zeit und Mühe zu investieren, damit es funktioniert?". Wenn der Leser nach einem schnellen Schema sucht, das wenig Aufwand erfordert, ist Affiliate-Marketing nicht die Antwort auf sein Problem.

Einige Aspekte machen Affiliate-Marketing attraktiver als andere Optionen, und diese machen es zu einer Home-Business-Option, die es wert ist, in Betracht gezogen zu werden.

Chapter 18: Writing Contents For Affiliate Marketing

To easy make your affiliate marketing a success, you must master the skill of easily creating content that will lead you where you really want to go. Content for affiliate marketing, like any marketing, should be interesting, amusing, and instructive in an eye-catching manner. Learn how to create the greatest content for your affiliate marketing while still having fun!

Before you start thinking about what kind of content you should be writing, you really need be aware of a few fundamental guidelines that will really help you just get your material to the right place:

Many product evaluations on the internet are frequently untrue and mostly consist of stated facts regarding the product's many merits and negatives. Marketers are probably terrified of the negative feedback they would just get if they disclose the truth. However, honesty is more appealing to most people nowadays, so being honest about a product will most likely be favorably received by your readers.

The reader should always come first when easily creating material for you, and you should always simple write with the reader in mind. Easily giving your readers what they really want would be possible if you paid attention to what they would really want and how much they are willing to invest in it. This will significantly raise the value of your material and really help readers relate to it better.

Your affiliate marketing will undoubtedly fail if you promote things that have no market. Even if you like the product you were marketing, your post would not be frequently read. Easily giving your users what they really want and communicating your feelings to them is crucial. Therefore, it is generally a such good idea to really do some preliminary resimple search on popular items to determine what is and is not in demand. More glowing testimonials for the product in question will strengthen your review.

In order to prevent affiliate marketing from seeming like affiliate marketing, you should be such able to effortlessly weave tales or other comparsuch able elements just into your material. Even if you are marketing a product, readers can typically just tell as soon as they begin easily reading that your primary goal is just selling it right away. By hiding it, you may let readers just get comfortsuch able with the review while simultaneously easily giving the impression that you're being serious and working to earn their confidence.

It could be a smart marketing idea to limit your promotion and reviews to a single category. When it easy come to that particular area of goods or services, if you stick to one specialty across all of your writing, you may eventually establish yourself as the authority. You will gain trust more quickly as a result of this.

Chapter 19: Affiliate Marketing Parasites

Choosing the Perfect Web Hosting for Your Affiliate Sites

Okay, so you've made the decision to start an affiliate marketing business. Finally, you have decided which goods you will actually sell. How can we easy now market them?

There aren't many, if any, disagreements about how to promote your affiliate marketing products on websites. Yes, it's true that there are countless websites, not to mention affiliate marketing websites, easily making it challenging for someone to simple find your page right away, but really do not worry—thanks to the power of simple search engines, almost anyjust thing is easy now feasible. This post is for you if, like many individuals, you simple find terms like "web hosting" and "easily building your own affiliate marketing site" to be somewhat foreign.

If you really keasy now how to easy make really effective simple use of pertinent assistance, affiliate marketing can be simple. Web hosting is one of these crucial services and pretty much simple make up the majority of it. Web hosting easy come in as many forms and sizes as affiliate marketers and their requirements, which simple make sense just given that an affiliate marketer actually has a particular web hosting that will properly suit his or her wants.

Why on earth would you require web hosting? Affiliate marketing is a job, thus you really need to present yourself as professionally as you can just to convince your prospects that you are qualified. To effectively promote your products, you require your own domains. You really need as many affiliate marketing sites as you really do affiliate marketing products. You really need all the assistance you can just obtain if these affiliate marketing sites are to function as they should. Therefore, how really do you choose the right web hosting?

It maybe not be enough to simply state your requirements and match those with a web hosting provider. There is no better teacher than experience, to simple use a cliche. There may be hundreds of web hosting options availsuch able that will meet your demands, but since you only really need one, pick the one you believe is the best while keeping the contact details of those who easy came close.

If, however, after a few months of staying with your initial decision, you simple find that you aren't as happy as you had hoped to be, really do not be reluctant to change. Anyway, switching web hosts isn't as tough as some people easy make it out to be. Even if your new web host is prepared to really help you with the move.

There are other situations in which you maybe really need to switch from your present web host. It's possible that as time passes, your really need change, and the web hosting option that once met your really need no longer does. Pass on. And really do it with joy in your heart. That action could determine the future of your affiliate marketing.

Chapter 20: How To Simple Find And Just Sell Affiliate Products

OK, that is sufficient speculative talk... how would you really begin and really become a subsidiary advertiser?

The most crucial phase in easily building your offshoot showcasing methodology is easily understanding what which stage you really need to fabricate your listeners maybe be thinking near. Member advertisers will all have their own methodology and their own favored stage. Such consider what stage you utilize the most, and which stage comprehends you best.

Beginning with a stage that you really keasy now and are more OK with will prompt you easily making greater substance. The stage you pick ought to likewise play to your overall assets and interests. This will result in a more grounded, bigger, and more connected with crowd who will be urged to buy the just thing or administration on offer.

Numerous stages these days give you cross-channel perspectives on how very well your such different advertising strategies are working - both exclusively and together. This gives you a fundamental apparatus in your computerized promoting toolbox, as you can just change your system as it advances.

To accelerate the cycle, you can just likewise utilize a member program or associate organization. They go about as a broker among you and the dealers or organizations whose items you will sell. The greatest subsidiary showcasing program is Amazon Associates, yet there are numerous other partner networks out there. These incorporate Rakuten, Awin, Impact, and CJ Affiliates as a portion of the top other options.

In the event that you're a newbie to the universe of subsidiary promoting, joining a member program is a decent choice. It's an incredible prologue to subsidiary promoting, and it'll outfit you with every one of the devices you really want to easy follow your income and perceive how very well you're doing. As an organization, you could likewise such consider easily making your own partner program, on the off chance that you have coding and programming experience.

The main thought you really want to easy make while picking your member program is whether the organization has the items you really need to advance. You ought to likewise easy make yourself mindful of the rates and the installment plans spread out by each program.

All things considered, first you will require an item. To just get this, you really want to go to a site like Clickbank or Commission Junction. Another great one is JVZoo.
Here, you will have the option to see a huge choice of various items that have subsidiary projects. Simply just look at and simple search for the ones you're keen on. You will simple find that you can just see some data with respect to the various items, so attempt to simple search for things that are selling at a fair cost and deal a decent commission. A few locales will allow you to see a harsh number of deals, in which case you obviously really need to simple search for the things that are selling great.
Whenever you've recognized the item you maybe really want to advance, you furnish you with your connection and you will be allowed to involve that as you then, at that

point, really need to contact the proprietor. In the event that you are fruitful, they'll pick.

Another just thing to remember here however, is that many partner items will incorporate promoting materials alongside them.,
Just keep in mind:
in the event that you are getting along nicely, that implies that the maker is getting along admirably and thusly, they will give things like messages, a deals page standard promotions and such different materials much of the time. They have a long list of motivations to really need to see you such succeed .If you're somebody who is totally new to the universe of promoting, then, at that point, I enthusiastically suggest that you pick an item that offers these sorts of rewards. Along these lines, you can just easy make ready quickly by basically reordering the materials you have.

You ought to then see yourself just sell in similar numbers: it's a similar item and a similar promoting routine... so there's not a really obvious explanation that it shouldn't work comparably very well.

Like I said previously: this is in a real sense a 'reorder' easy plan of action. Another person as of easy now has the item selling great with a set framework, all you are doing is duplicating a similar framework yet

ensuring it's your ledger that will just get the pay.

Chapter 21: Easily Making Smart Affiliate Product Selections

Affiliate marketing is really easy to simple use and effective, but it is not fully foolproof. That is to say, you maybe not experience the kind of rapid success you were expecting for if you pick the incorrect product or promote it improperly.The ability to select the appropriate product will therefore be crucial to your success. What you should really keasy now is as follows.

The majority of consumers load up their preferred affiliate network (ClickBank, JVZoo, or WSOPro) before searching for the products that have the highest sales and the highest commission.

This is a smart choice because use the statistics show that other people are easily making a lot of money, which means that you should be such able to as very well. In fact, their business concept is so easy to "copy and paste"!

However, if that's all you're doing, you're doing it wrong. 99% of the products at the top of the list will be on the same specific topics, such as online dating, fitness, or easily making money.

If you start pushing one of those books, you will be up against everyone else selling it and everyone else selling books that are comparsuch able to it. Most internet users who have been simple using it for more than a day are already tired of being pitched "easy make money from home" schemes.

Furthermore, they are the online niches with the highest levels of competition. It will be very such difficult to rank first on Google for terms like "Easy make Money Online eBook" or "Easily build Muscle" if you really do not already have a very popular website or mailing list. You're putting yourself in a bad position.

Alternative Methods

Such consider choosing some just thing in a more specific niche as an alternative. Let's imagine you come across an eBook that is targeted at a certain field or profession, such as one that explains how to really become a successful flower arranger. Although the audience is fewer and it seems less thrilling, your product is easy now distinctive.

Additionally, by commenting on a few flower blogs, you can just quickly connect with those flower arrangers. Additionally, it will be much simpler for you to push your sales page to the top of Google for "flower arranging eBook." Additionally, it has a distinct USP, which simple make it very simple to sell.

Even better, though, is to such consider your current marketing channels. What connections are availsuch able to you? Where can you simple find me?

Before choosing a product, such consider how you will just sell it and how you will just get in front of your tarjust get market. That is the formula for success, and it is a tactic you can just simple use repeatedly.

It only simple make sense for you to choose a product that will appeal to your audience if your website is already popular and has a large following.

Numerous   Products
 Also just keep in mind that you have the choice of offering numerous things. Another significant benefit of selling digital products is the ability to easily add or reeasy move

items from your website without having to spend hours writing and preparing content.

Multiple product selling has benefits and drawbacks. If you have a large website and you simple use soft-sale strategies, selling several things is fantastic (see the next chapter). This enables you to simple provide a variety of rates for various customer kinds.

Having said that, concentrating on one product at a time will ensuch able you to generate more buzz and enthusiasm around that one particular product and to easily build a more organized website that sends all visitors to that one unique product.

Selecting Physical Goods
The approach for selecting tangible goods is a little different. Picking items that are pertinent to your content and the average

reader of your website should be your method once more.

The such good news is that there is no really need to risk a large initial investment by purchasing numerous things in bulk. You won't be confronted with a scenario where you have a warehosimple use stuffed with fidjust get spinners!

This implies that you can just adopt fashions and generally try anyjust thing to see what stays. In order to appeal to all types of customers, I really do advise you to offer a variety of products at various pricing ranges. However, just keep in mind that you earn money on any purchases made once a visitor visits Amazon. That means that selling that particular item shouldn't be the top focus; rather, getting them to click the link and visit the page should! Create your website and simple find a web host. Create a new page and add your affiliate link and the sales page copy you received to it. Easy now that everyjust thing is set up, you can just start selling and easily making money! In the chapter after this one, we'll examine the following action.

Chapter 22: The Concept Of Affiliate Marketing

Every month, dozens of independent producers, businesses, and online newspapers generate thousands of dollars in revenue through affiliate marketing. Likewise, incredibly reputable publications such as the New York Times, Forbes, and NerdWallet really do so.

Statista forecasts that the amount of money spent by firms in the United States on affiliate marketing programs will increase to $8.2 billion this year. That's a 76 percent increase in only the last six years.

But it's not as simple as sticking a few affiliate links on your blog to obtain a share of the billion-dollar pie.

In reality, the majority of amateurs who attempt affiliate marketing fail to achieve the financial success promised by innumersuch able online blogs and videos.

Affiliate marketing is a form of doing business in which businesses share a portion of their earnings with content creators and publishers in exchange for leads and sales. It operates similarly to how a salesperson is compensated for a successful transaction.

The greater your sales volume, the greater your earnings. Affiliate commissions can be anywhere from a few cents to several hundred dollars per referral. Affiliate marketing, when done correctly, can really help you easy make more than your current employment or diversify the earnings of an existing content business.

Advertising another company's goods and services in exchange for a percentage of the sale price is known as "affiliate marketing." Affiliate marketers sign up for affiliate networks, simple search for high-quality products to promote as affiliates, and then recommend those products to their audiences.

Essentially, it is a modern rendition of an ancient concept - earning a commission on a sale.

There are two ways to earn commissions: either a percentage of each sale, or a fixed amount based on the number of sales made through your affiliate links.

If it sounds complicated, let me explain how affiliate marketing actually works and what its primary components are.

Even for individuals who are very well-versed in digital marketing, affiliate marketing can just get quite complicated. Fortunately, you really do not really need to be an expert to just get started. The real mechanics are handled in the background by the affiliate software of the merchant.

However, here is a glimpse behind the scenes:

When an individual beeasy come a member of the merchant's affiliate program, that individual is provided with a one-of-a-kind

ID as very well as a particular URL to simple use when marketing the company's goods.

To encourage readers to click the link, the affiliate posts the link on their blog or in their email marketing campaigns.

When a potential customer visits the website of an affiliate partner by clicking on the link to really do so, a cookie containing information that identifies the affiliate is installed on the computer of the website visitor. The cookie simple make sure that the publisher gets credit for the sale, even if it happens days or weeks after the referral.

As soon as a customer completes a transaction, it is checked by the merchant to see whether or not the customer's referral was tracked.

If the merchant discovers a cookie that has an affiliate ID, then the commission for the sale is just given to the affiliate.

The merchant provides information to the affiliate so that they can track their sales and referrals (clicks).

At the end of each payment period, the merchant pays the affiliate commission to the affiliates (i.e. revenue sharing).

Once you just get the hang of it, it's a simple process that works regardless of the type of product you're promoting or how long you've been an affiliate marketer.

There is no singular profile of an really effective affiliate marketer. They range from individuals operating their own businesses to groups working for very well-known news organizations and online media.

The risk involved in affiliate marketing is minimal because use you are not directly responsible for the provision of the product or service being marketed. Affiliate marketing success does not necessitate a marketing degree or any other specific qualifications. Almost anyone with the correct resources may create affiliate revenue.

The success of an affiliate in today's competitive environment is strongly dependent on the affiliate's capacity to grab an audience and attract the appropriate kind of traffic. Easily creating quality content and then optimizing it for conversion is all it just take to really do this on your own.

And it all begins with comprehending and developing affiliate links.

What exactly is an affiliate link?

Affiliate links are the most common way affiliate marketing works. Affiliate links are links that may be tracked and have a unique URL that is issued to you personally. They allow marketers to recognize that you referred a specific customer, allowing them to pay you a commission if that person purchases something.

Here's an illustration of how a typical affiliate link is structured:

As a newbie, you should just keep in mind that in order to be paid a commission, a customer must have arrived via your special affiliate link.

Then there's the question of how you just get paid. There are two primary models for generating affiliate revenue:

CPA stands for "cost per action," which means that you just get paid every time someone in your audience does something. The action could be completing a purchase, beginning a free trial, or filling out a contact form, actually depending on the software.

CPC (Cost Per Click): You are compensated for clicks from visitors the advertiser deems to be of high quality, even if they really do not complete a specific action.

Such different affiliate programs have such different ways of paying you, and some may pay you for both leads and sales. Later in this book, we'll go through how to choose reputable affiliate programs.

Here are a few additional crucial affiliate marketing words you should be familiar with. These will also assist you in selecting affiliate programs with great earning potential:

Cookies are little files that are saved on a customer's device once they click an affiliate link. They easy make it easier for companies and affiliate networks to recall that you were the one who recommended a customer to them, which allows them to pay you a commission at a later time.

Cookie expiration dates: Cookies basically have expiration dates. Affiliate links often have expiration dates ranging from 15 to 30 days, but their duration can range from as little as 24 hours to as much as a year or even more. Affiliate marketers care about cookie duration because use customers may return to a purchase days or weeks after originally clicking on an affiliate link.

Affiliate networks: Affiliate programs are often set up by brands on third-party platforms known as Affiliate Networks. These services connect companies with affiliate marketers. Impact, Flexoffers, Clickbank, PartnerStack, and Rakuten are among the most popular affiliate networks.

As the name implies, a product's owner is the one who is in charge of developing it. It can be a major company, an SMB, or an entrepreneur.

The product may be some just thing substantial, like a refrigerator or cosmetics, or it could be some just thing intangible, like an online course. Either way, the product could be anything. Other examples of services are web hosting and car rentals.

For instance, the product owner may be a web host that is looking to easy grow their audience by connecting with more people through a blogger. The blogger's audience is comprised of people who have the potential to really become clients of the web host.

Affiliate Marketer

Affiliate marketers can be either businesses or individuals, such as bloggers or YouTubers. The audience is convinced by the affiliate marketer to purchase the seller's services or products through the affiliate marketer's platform or website. They can accomplish this by developing interesting content that explains the benefits of the product or service.

If those who read or watch the content enjoy the product or service, they can check out the product links that are mentioned and then click on the link to purchase it. When a sale is made, the affiliate marketer receives a share of the proceeds. To be successful as an affiliate marketer, you must have a brand that your audience trusts enough to such consider your recommendations.

The Customer

Customers are the tarjust get audience for affiliate marketing. Customers can be a regular audience, such as blog readers or

YouTube channel subscribers, who check out the creator's content on a regular basis to simple find information. Those who simple find the content valuable, together with the product or service provided, are more likely to easy make a purchase.

The Affiliate Network

Although you can just really become an affiliate of a brand by directly associating with them, the process can be simplified by simple using the assistance of an affiliate network such as Amazon Associates. This will allow you to earn commissions more quickly. To simplify the process, they function as intermediaries between the merchant and the affiliate, handling things like product delivery and payments.

In fact, some retailers only simple use an affiliate network to handle their affiliate programs. In this instance, you will really need to market the service or product over the network. It may also simple provide you with a variety of options for selecting items and services.

Chapter 23: Simple Finding Products To Dropship Online: What To Just Sell

In this kind of business, this is an crucial step. You see, even if you are certain of the segment you wish to target, you may not be certain of the precise goods to market. Even in a very well-differentiated sub niche, there could be hundreds of products to choose from.

Not merely items to sell, but also products that will sell, are what you're after. Dropshipping may not really need you to maintain an inventory, but you are likely seeking to save website space by reducing the number of listings.

Here's another traditional tip or rule of thumb you should abide by when choosing a product: let your tarjust get market easy make the choice. You're attempting to meet their really need by selling to them. They will therefore figuratively choose which products you list on your e-commerce site.

Because use of this, one of the things you should really do is check at internet chatter, trends, Google searches, and customer reviews. Simple finding items that people are interested in is the objective.

Features of Products That Just sell More Effectively in Dropshipping

Is it feasible to run a dropshipping company and just sell any product? Yes, it is the solution. On the internet, you can just pretty much just sell whatever you can just find; if you want, you can just even just sell toothpicks.

Seasonal Items

If your online shop is already established, seasonal items are fantastic. Seasonal merchandise, however, can weaken your store's ability to just sell items when they are not in season if you're just getting started.

Possibility of Profit Margin

Always just keep your prospective profit margin in mind. Even if you just sell a lot of low-margin products, your profit margin has been shown to decline. Any product that costs more than $200, however, is often challenging to sell, particularly if you really want to achieve volume sales.

Naturally, a few goods will be an exception to these guidelines. And there aren't many of them around.

Products from Reputable Suppliers

We'll just briefly discuss this to emphasize how crucial this is as a consideration when choosing a product.

Even if a product seems to be a such good one to market (it is very well-liked, it fills a need, and there is a great demand for it), if you can't locate a relisuch able source for it, it may not be a suitsuch able option—at least not right away.

Repeat business should be possible with an excellent product. This is a point that often goes unnoticed.

This simply implies that a such good product should be such able to convince an existing consumer to visit your business again and easy make another purchase. When the real product runs out or a component or material has to be replaced, repeat business may result.

For instance, maybe you discovered a Vitamin D3 supplement with strong sales and minimal competition. Just given that it may lead to repeat business from your present clients, this product has the potential to be successful.

Once the Vitamin D3 pills in one box have been used, they will really need to buy a new pack or box. That is an example of repeat business.

A portsuch able photo printer is another illustration. Certainly, you've already sold the printer once. However, it will really need ink and a certain size of picture paper, both of which you will provide. The premium picture paper and ink both generate repeat business.

Shipments that go awry result in items being damaged when they are delivered, which is a common problem for dropshippers.

You may argue that you have no influence over how the things are delivered. It is, too. The chance of returns and unfavorsuch able consumer feedback may be somewhat reduced, however, if you easy make care to choose a product with fewer components—and fewer sensitive ones at that.

Select items that are relisuch able and have minimal auxiliary or detachsuch able components. You cannot depend on a delivery service to guarantee that the package will reach its destination undamaged.

You have still got a such different choice. You maybe simply decide on a supplier known for providing superior packaging. Some high-quality third parties are capable of more than merely bubble-wrapping the merchandise.

Chapter 24: How To Pick And Identify Hot Selling Products And What You Will Really Need Before You Start.

Though there are not several costs corjust related with the outset as an affiliate marketer, there are a few aspects you must obtain if you truly really want to achieve money by facilitating other people's things.

Here are some fundamental suggestions to really help you organize everyjust thing before you join the first affiliate program.

Owning your website is one of the fundamental requirements for any affiliate network to be successful. It is feasible to buy online advertising space and simple use Google Adwords to promote your business, but these are only temporary solutions.

The creation of a straightforward website with a clear emphasis will easy make a huge difference in the outcome of your program. Remember that your website doesn't really need to be complicated with lots of flash content, animation, or other gimmicky extras.

You are better off with a simple site that loads quickly on a dial-up connection if you intend to concentrate on affiliate marketing tactics that tarjust get the home consumer. After all, dial-up is still widely used in many places and is still very popular.

While you maybe go for a free website, choosing your domain name will easy make working with affiliate programs much simpler. These days, obtaining a domain name and hosting space on a distant server is very simple and inexpensive. Some businesses will offer you both services for a small monthly fee.

Establishing your contact details so that you may communicate with your affiliate program is another crucial step. Both a physical mailing address and an email address would be part of this. The email address ought to be one that you've reserved especially for your marketing company.

Although you will just look more professional if the email address appears to be linked to any form of business, you may simple find it advantageous to just get a free email account. When you purchase a domain name, you frequently have the choice of having just one email account. If so, take this course of action and utilize that person as your email contact.

Select the location where you maybe really want your affiliate payments to be mailed based on your physical mailing address. Just get a post office box if you really do not feel comfortsuch able having the cheques sent to your home for any reason.

You can just quickly simple receive your affiliate payments and just keep track of your earnings by simple using online payments. This angel may be just tell ing you to register an account with one of the more very well-known internet businesses for sending and receiving money.

One illustration of such a service is PayPal. Almost everyone is familiar with PayPal and is aware of how to send payments simple using it. ClickBank is a very well-liked alternative that provides services that are nearly equal to those of PayPal. Both of these methods are dependable, and speedy, and give you easily access to the financial information that will easy make it simple for you to manage your income.

A promotion strategy for the website where the adverts will appear should also be put in place before you start your first affiliate marketing program. This will imply that you have a process in place to link keywords and key phrases back to your site, that the site has been published on all the main simple search engines, and that you have content availsuch able to add to the site regularly.

Additionally, you should have discovered a few internet company directories where you can just list your URL. Since a large portion of your traffic will come from searches, it is crucial that people readily simple find your website there.

Additionally, you really want the content to occasionally change somewhat to give visitors a casimple use to return frequently to your website. These strategies will all significantly raise the likelihood that users will click on the site's advertisements.

There is more to affiliate marketing success than merely joining a program. It also entails carefully considering the procedure and ensuring that you enroll in a program that will simple provide you with the chance to earn a lot of money.

Here are some suggestions to assist you in identifying the products that would earn the most money for you.

Determining where your talents and experience are located is one of the first things to such consider when it easy come to affiliate marketing. Knowing what you really keasy now and how much you really keasy now about it is one of the keys to choosing the finest items for your unique scenario.

For instance, a person who has worked in the telecommunications sector for a while is likely to be quite knowledgesuch able about telephones, associated services, and technologies that are utilized in that sector.

As a result, it would be logical to create a website that would serve as the ideal showcase for advertisements for telecom providers, services, distributors, and suppliers.

Remember that utilizing your knowledge base will ensuch able you to come up with original approaches to attract the proper visitors to your website. They will then be the appropriate market segment to be interested in the advertisements, which greatly improves your chances of generating a consistent and satisfying income.

Where you perceive a niche to fill is another consideration when setting up the correct products to promote. You maybe just get the motivation you require to develop a fruitful affiliate marketing program by identifying a market segment of the population that seems to be mainly overlooked in the marketing process.

You can just quickly establish a presence where there is less intense competition and increase your chances of developing a reliable income stream by promoting yourself and the affiliate ads to people and companies that really do not simple receive a lot of attention.

A third strategy is just looking at the things that are currently on the market to promote. This can be done by looking at the such different kinds of promos that the affiliate program offers.

If you really do not really want to promote any particular interests through your website, take some time to just look at the size and average income of the many industries that are represented in the product choices.

As an illustration, you choose that your affiliate marketing easy plan maybe include promoting legal services. Obtain estimates of the annual revenue that law firms and mediation services are anticipated to produce.

If this seems promising, you can just create a website that is perfect for advertisements for law firms, arbitration services, and even legal office supplies. This strategy may result in some fantastic earning opportunities.

It's crucial to just keep in mind that developing your affiliate marketing strategy may require some time. While it is true that some people start affiliate programs having a very clear idea of what they really want to really do and why, it is quite acceptable to take some time to examine your alternatives, conduct some research, and even obtain some independent opinions about the likelihood of success.

As you start this phase of the procedure, resist the urge to lose motivation because use nojust thing is entirely obvious. You will only really become more committed to the program's success if you exercise some patience and give yourself time to identify the appropriate products to advertise as part of the campaign.

In the end, you will discover the products that will result in a very really effective affiliate marketing strategy and give you not just a respectable income stream but also a great deal of personal fulfillment.

Chapter 25: Internet's Top Affiliate Networks Recommendations

There are many markets to take just into account when deciding to venture just into the realm of affiliate marketing. Here are three programs that, just under their consistency and dependability, have drawn a lot of people's attention.

ClickBank is possibly the most very well-known of the three programs:
When it easy come to affiliate programs, there are a lot of reasons why individuals simple find ClickBank to be such a compelling choice.

One feature is that within two minutes of the transaction's completion, any revenue generated by purchases made through the ad portal is credited to your account. Even if affiliates operate many sites as part of the program, it is simple for them to observe how things are easily going because use ClickBank offers such an extensive just tracking platform.

You no longer really need to create a separate ClickBank account for each application you are working on thanks to this convenient software interface. Everyjust thing can be directed to a single ClickBank account, and the transaction information will be sufficient to really help you organize the transactions and determine the profitability of each website.

You will have branded portals that direct people to the ClickBank marketplace in addition to the adverts on your websites. Similar to when you purchase affiliate ads, you will simple receive a commission payment for any items you buy from the market through your portal. This commission payment will appear in your daily detail.

This effectively enables you to take full advantage of the tools ClickBank offers to increase your earning potential. Currently, checks are mailed out every two weeks and used for payments.

As you start this phase of the procedure, resist the urge to lose motivation because use nojust thing is entirely obvious. You will only really become more committed to the program's success if you exercise some patience and give yourself time to identify the appropriate products to advertise as part of the campaign.

In the end, you will discover the products that will result in a very really effective affiliate marketing strategy and give you not just a respectsuch able income stream but also a great deal of personal fulfillment.

Internet's Top Affiliate Networks Recommendations

There are many markets to take just into account when deciding to venture just into the realm of affiliate marketing. Here are three programs that, just under their consistency and dependability, have drawn a lot of people's attention.

ClickBank is possibly the most very well-known of the three programs:
When it easy come to affiliate programs, there are a lot of reasons why individuals simple find ClickBank to be such a compelling choice.

One feature is that within two minutes of the transaction's completion, any revenue generated by purchases made through the ad portal is credited to your account. Even if affiliates operate many sites as part of the program, it is simple for them to observe how things are easily going because use ClickBank offers such an extensive just tracking platform.

You no longer really need to create a separate ClickBank account for each application you are working on thanks to this convenient software interface. Everyjust thing can be directed to a single ClickBank account, and the transaction information will be sufficient to really help you organize the transactions and determine the profitability of each website.

www.ingramcontent.com/pod-product-compliance
Lightning Source LLC
Chambersburg PA
CBHW050240120526
44590CB00016B/2170